NATURE'S BEST HUNTERS

TOM JACKSON

HOW ANIMALS BECOME
THE MOST POWERFUL PREDATORS

{CONTENTS}

EVOLUTION

This bamboo pit viper has heat-sensitive patches on its snout. These patches can detect the body heat of prey even when it is hiding among leaves.

Evolution is the process by which living things can change gradually. Over millions of years, many tiny changes add up to some big differences. Evolution is why there are so many different species living on Earth. Some species are obviously more closely related than others. In 1859, Charles Darwin said that related species had evolved from the same ancestor in the past. He explained how evolution could do that with a process called natural selection.

Animals in a species may look the same, but they all have a unique set of variations. These differences make some animals 'fitter' than others. The fitter ones are better at surviving in wild conditions. Darwin said that nature 'selects' these fit animals; they have many children, while the unfit ones die off. Over time, the characteristics that make an animal fit become more common, and eventually every member of the species has it – the species has evolved a tiny bit.

It is not just the way animals look that can evolve. Natural selection also changes the way they behave. The creatures in this book have evolved to be successful hunters. Some powerful hunters are able to catch almost any other animal that lives nearby. Other predators are specialists and are the best at catching just one type of prey, but everything else is out of their reach. Of course, for every predator there is always a prey, and the evolution of hunting skills occurs at the same time as the evolution of methods of escaping from hunters. As we will see, nature's best hunters use an amazing range of techniques to get hold of their food!

The king cobra is one of the largest and deadliest snakes. When it rises up with its hood fanned out, it is warning us that it is about to dart forwards and bite. Most animals flee, but the mongoose stands and fights. This frisky little hunter is fast enough to leap out of the way of the cobra's fangs and bite the snake back at lightning speed. Despite the cobra's venom being powerful enough to kill an elephant, the mongoose will eventually win this battle to the death.

GREAT WHITE SHARK

Why is the white shark so great? Simply because it is the largest and most powerful hunting fish on the planet. The shark can grow to longer than a minibus and it uses an array of super-senses to track its prey. They never see it coming for the kill.

A great white shark hunts in deep, open water. The first clue it gets about where to find some food comes from its ears. The shark can pick up the sounds of an animal splashing from 250m away. Once it turns in that direction, the nose takes over. A third of the shark's brain is devoted to sensing smells, and it can pick up the equivalent of a teaspoon of blood dropped in a swimming pool.

A great white's teeth often fall out during attacks. Any lost teeth are replaced very quickly, however. Great whites can grow up to 3,000 teeth in a lifetime!

This great white has attacked with such force, it has leapt out of the water.

FACTS AND FIGURES

Scientific name...Carcharodon carcharias
Location.. Worldwide
Habitat... Oceans
Size..4m
Food........................Seals, fish, seabirds
Lifespan....................................30 years
Young.. Pups born

Splashing tells the shark that an animal is nearby, blood reveals that it is in trouble. Perhaps there are other sharks feeding, and there may be more food to go around.

The great white's favourite food is sea lion. These sea mammals swim close to the surface, and from down deep the shark can see their silhouettes against the pale surface of the water. The shark normally attacks from behind. As it approaches, the shark rolls its eyes into its head to protect them in the fight to come. The shark's first bite is just to taste the prey. If it tastes good and blubbery, the shark will, clamp its jaws around its meal and drag it under water.

The shark's nose has electrical sensors that guide it to targets in the dark.

EVOLUTION SOLUTION

The great white shark has been hunting in the oceans for 150 million years. It evolved long before the sea lion – its main food today. To start with, great whites hunted big fish, swimming reptiles and even ocean-going crocodiles. However, they can use their hunting system to attack just about anything. So while new prey has evolved, these sharks have not had to evolve new hunting techniques.

Great whites very seldomly eat humans. They may bite them, but normally spit them out because their flesh isn't very fatty.

MANTIS SHRIMP

This 15-cm crustacean punches its prey to death. It has the fastest punch of any animal, and is able to create a force that is as powerful as a bullet fired from a small pistol.

The mantis shrimp lives mostly alone, on the seabed around coral reefs. If two mantis shrimps meet, they will fight using the sharp spear-like weapons on their front legs. Some species hunt with these spears, too, but others use a much more powerful weapon to kill prey. Their front legs are hefty clubs, which are locked into a folded position. To catch prey, the shrimp tenses the muscles in its club until it unlocks and flies outwards. The club hits prey at 80km/h and smashes it into little pieces.

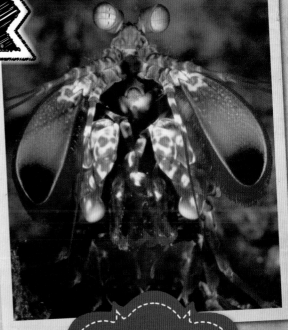

Mantis shrimps can see heat, colours and UV light. They are able to focus on six things at once!

The shock wave formed by a mantis shrimp's punch is enough to rip a hole in the water, leaving a vacuum. As the vacuum collapses, sparks of electricity and even flashes of light are formed.

FACTS AND FIGURES

Scientific name	Stomatopoda
Location	Worldwide
Habitat	Coral reefs
Size	10–35cm
Food	Crabs, prawns
Lifespan	5 years
Young	Eggs protected in burrow

EVOLUTION SOLUTION

Predators and prey are in an evolutionary 'arms race'. Prey animals are always evolving ways of escaping from predators, and predators are always evolving ways of catching prey more easily. This arms race led to the mantis shrimp's record-breaking punch, which evolved to crack open the armoured shells used by crabs as defence from attack.

NILE CROCODILE

The crocodile has the most powerful bite in the animal kingdom. This hunter uses its jaws to grab prey in a crushing bite and drag it under water to drown. However, its huge jaw cannot chew food, which makes eating prey a lot more complicated.

Nile crocodiles are the biggest reptiles in Africa. They live in the shallow rivers, often lurking motionless by the bank waiting for prey to come to the water's edge to drink or wade across to the other side. With a flick of its long, paddle-like tail, the crocodile lunges forward and clamps its jaw on to its victim. If that does not kill it straight away, the crocodile pulls the animal down into deep water and waits for it to drown.

Being bitten by a Nile crocodile is like being squashed by a two tonne weight.

EVOLUTION SOLUTION

A crocodile's jaw muscles evolved to be very good at pulling the mouth shut in a big bite. However, the muscles that make it open again are very weak. This is why human crocodile hunters are able to tie the animal's mouth closed – it is too weak to break the string. The muscle system is also why crocodiles cannot chew. They never evolved the necessary muscles. Instead, they twist off chunks of flesh and swallow them whole.

The Nile crocodile is quite slow on land, but can out-swim its prey in water – this gazelle does not stand a chance.

FACTS AND FIGURES

Scientific name....	Crocodylus niloticus
Location	Africa
Habitat	Rivers
Size	4.2m
Food	Fish, antelopes, water birds
Lifespan	100 years
Young	Eggs buried in sand

KINGFISHER

As its name suggests, the colourful kingfisher is among nature's top bird hunters. This shy bird spends a lot of the time just sitting and looking at the river water passing beneath it. But when it spots a fish below, it dives into action, and seldom misses.

The bird sweeps back its wings like an arrow to help its body slice through the water.

The kingfisher lives along the edge of clear woodland rivers with shallow bottoms. It uses a branch that extends over the water as its lookout position. Its eyes are very powerful and can see small silver fish, such as sticklebacks, flitting about in the water below. However, water plays tricks on the eyes by bending light a little, so an object appears in a slightly different place to where it actually is. The kingfisher solves this problem by having an oily lens in each eye that corrects the position. As it enters the water, the bird switches to using another part of each eye to keep track of the target.

Male kingfishers are blue and gold, while females have more green feathers.

FACTS AND FIGURES

Scientific name.............. Alcedo atthisi

Location....... Europe, Asia, North Africa

Habitat........................ Woodland rivers

Size...45cm

Food...Fish

Lifespan.....................................7 years

Young... 5 eggs laid in riverbank burrow

Wet feathers are much heavier than dry ones, so take-off from the water is very hard work. The bird will use its beak to comb its feathers dry when it reaches its perch.

EVOLUTION SOLUTION

The water's edge is a good place to hunt. The kingfisher lives outside of its prey's habitat, so fish are less likely to know it is there. The element of surprise helps the bird to be such a successful hunter. Crocodiles use the same trick, just with the prey being out of its habitat, so in the water.

The bird dives headfirst into the water and plunges to a depth of up to 50cm to snatch the fish in its long pointed beak. The kingfisher must now swim up to the surface and flap its wings hard to get back into the air. Back on the branch, the bird always eats the fish head-first. This way, none of the fish's spikes get stuck in its throat.

GREEN ANACONDA

This South American species is the biggest snake in the world. Once caught in its coils, no animal gets out alive. Even other big hunters, such as the caiman and jaguar, are not safe!

Green anacondas do not need much energy to survive. An adult survive on one big meal a year!

EVOLUTION SOLUTION

The green anaconda is the largest living snake; other species are longer but none are as heavy. The anaconda's great size and strength evolved to match that of its prey. Many of its prey are hunters themselves, such as jaguars and caimans. Being so large also means anacondas use energy very efficiently, surviving for months on one catch.

It is sometimes said that anacondas crush their prey to death. That is not true, they simply stop them being able to breathe so that they die of suffocation.

FACTS AND FIGURES

Scientific name.......... Eunectes murinus
Location........................... South America
Habitat.................Forests and wetlands
Size... 6–9m
Food................... Deer, capybara, caimans
Lifespan.....................................10 years
Young............. 30 young born each year

The green anaconda has a lot of sharp teeth for gripping prey, but the snake does not have a venomous bite. Instead, it kills by constriction. The snake wraps its huge, muscled body around its prey. As the prey struggles free from one coil, the snake just wraps more around it. Eventually, the victim's neck and body is held tight by the snake. When the prey breathes out, the snake tightens its grip slightly, and that makes it harder for its victim to breathe in again. Eventually, the prey cannot breathe at all and is suffocated to death. Then, the snake stretches its mouth around the dead animal's head and gradually swallows it whole!

VELVET WORM

The velvet worm will bite a hole in its prey and pump in its stomach juices. This digests the prey into a liquid, which the velvet worm can slurp up.

Velvet worms are a peculiar group of animals. They have long bodies like a worm, but also have several legs and clawed feet which makes them more like centipedes. Plus, they kill prey with glue!

FACTS AND FIGURES

Scientific name................. Onychophora
Location................ Southern Hemisphere
Habitat................................... Rainforests
Size..5cm
Food....................... Insects and worms
Lifespan............................... 6 years
Young .... 30 babies born each year

Some kinds of velvet worms give birth to young, which grow inside the mother's two wombs.

Velvet worms are named after the rings of soft scaly skin that cover their body. They live on the floors of tropical forests, where they hunt for snails, worms, beetles and centipedes. They hunt at night, using their antennae to pick up the smells of their prey. Once it finds a victim, the worm lifts up its head and squirts two jets of slime from glands on either side of its mouth. This slime dries quickly in the air to make a sticky goo that tangles with the prey's legs. Within seconds, the prey is helpless.

EVOLUTION SOLUTION

The ancestors of velvet worms lived on the ocean floor more than 500 million years ago. However, ancient marine velvet worms did not have the slime glands today's velvet worms use to catch prey. This is one of the reasons why marine velvet worms have long been extinct while the land-based ones have been around for hundreds of millions of years.

JAGUAR

The jaguar of South America is not as big as its cousins — the lions and tigers. However, this hunter's jaw has evolved to deliver the strongest bite of any cat — it can crush bones and an even crack skulls!

POLAR BEAR

The polar bear's scientific name means 'bear of the sea'. This is because it spends most of its time at sea – on the frozen Arctic Ocean. Polar bears only feed in summer, and have to walk and swim huge distances to find enough food before the winter comes.

A polar bear's favourite food is the ringed seal. These seals hunt for fish under the ice, and come to the surface to breathe every few minutes through holes in the ice. This is where the polar bear lies in wait. The bear can smell the seal as

EVOLUTION SOLUTION

Polar bears evolved from brown bears that came looking for food in the icy Arctic. The bears that had paler fur were more successful and eventually a new species of white bear evolved which could hide among ice. The bears' genes show that white fur evolved around 400,000 years ago.

FACTS AND FIGURES

Scientific name........ Ursus maritimus
Location.................................... Arctic
Habitat........................... Snow and ice
Size... 2.4–3m
Food........................... Seals, birds, deer
Lifespan.................................... 25 years
Young.................. 2 cubs born in winter

This polar bear has smelled a seal under the ice, and is about to punch a hole to catch its prey.

its head comes out of the water. The bear wastes no time leaping to attack. It uses its long, hooked claws to grab the seal and pull it out of the water. One blow from the bear's huge paw is enough to kill the seal. The bear can also smell seals resting under the ice. The bear rears up on its back legs and hammers down with its front paws, smashing its way into the seal's hideout in seconds.

ANGLERFISH

The anglerfish hunts in the dark, in the deep sea or on the gloomy seabed where there is hardly any light. However, the fish has got a light of its own, and uses it to lure smaller fish to their doom.

With its huge mouth lined with spiked teeth, the anglerfish looks a bit like a sea monster. However, it is impossible to see it in its natural habitat, as it is so dark there, and the water is completely black. Many animals that live down in the gloomy depths make their own light. Tiny jellyfish do it to signal to each other, so they can find mates. Anglerfish also make their own light, which glows and flashes from an organ on the end of a stalk that grows out of the fish's head.

The rest of the anglerfish's body apart from the stalk is black, so it is invisible in the dark.

Smaller fish mistake this light for the twinkles produced by jellyfish or other food. When they swim over to investigate, all they find is the monstrous killer fish, which looms out of the darkness and gobbles them up!

FACTS AND FIGURES

Scientific name................. Lophiiformes
Location..................................... Worldwide
Habitat................ Deep sea and seabeds
Size.. 10cm–1m
Food................................ Fish and shrimps
Lifespan................................. 20 years
Young........................ Sheets of eggs laid
                                        in rocky crevices

EVOLUTION SOLUTION

There are no plants in the deep sea because it is too dark for them to grow there. However, animals, such as anglerfish, have evolved to live in the deep and dark. Without plants, the non-hunting animals have evolved to eat another food source called 'marine snow'. This is the dead remains of animals and plants from higher up that sink down to the bottom of the sea.

17

JUMPING SPIDER

The jumping spider is as close as hunters get to being a superhero. This tiny spider can leap huge distances as it launches itself at prey. It also has massive eyes that fill most of its head – and it has a total of eight of them!

Jumping spiders are very deadly hunters. They kill with a fast-acting venom that damages nerves and paralyses a victim in an instant. The prey may not die straightaway, but the jumping spider will start to eat it anyway. Despite this fearsome ability, jumping spiders pose no threat to humans or any large animals. Most are 4mm long and their fangs are too tiny to puncture the skin of much larger animals.

The main eyes are tube-shaped, and stretch back far into the head. The other six eyes are much smaller and are used to detect shadows passing overhead that might signal danger.

A jumping spider pounces on an unsuspecting fly.

FACTS AND FIGURES

Scientific name......................Salticidae
Location.................................Worldwide
Habitat..............Woodlands, grasslands, deserts
Size.......................................1–22mm
Food...Insects
Lifespan...1 year
Young................100 eggs carried in sac

However, something the size of a beetle or fly would never see an attack coming. The jumping spider has two large forward-facing eyes that can swivel sideways to track prey in great detail. When it is ready, the spider springs forward using its long back legs, flying through the air and landing on its target; it never misses.

The spider cannot chew food, so once the prey is paralysed, the spider pumps stomach juices into its body. These turn the prey's body into liquid, so even if it was not quite dead, it soon will be. The spider then sucks up the fleshy goo, leaving the prey's empty husk.

Before leaping into the air, the spider ties on a safety line made of silk. This will stop it and its prey falling to the ground.

EVOLUTION SOLUTION

Spiders belong to a group of animals called chelicerates. These also include scorpions and ticks. Chelicerates have two spikey mouthparts; these are a spider's fangs. Insects are not chelicerates and they have many mouthparts working together to chew, bite and slice food. Spiders cannot do this and must eat liquid foods. The reason for the difference goes back almost 600 million years.

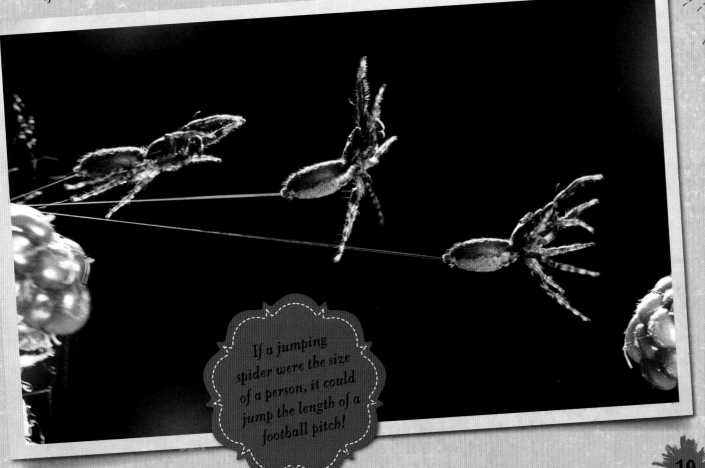

If a jumping spider were the size of a person, it could jump the length of a football pitch!

PEREGRINE FALCON

A peregrine falcon in a stoop travels faster than a passenger jet at take off.

This bird is the fastest animal on Earth, or at least the fastest animal above Earth! The falcon is a bird killer, and rockets down out of the sky to snatch its prey in mid-air.

The peregrine falcon is the most widespread bird of prey. Its natural habitat is any area with steep cliffs, which it shares with its favourite food, the rock pigeon. Pigeons live in the world's cities as well, and a skyscraper, or other tall building, makes a good artificial cliff for a peregrine falcon. The falcon perches at its nest on a high ledge, and when it sees a flock of birds approaching it takes to the air, flying high above its victims. Then it enters a

Aeroplane engineers have calculated the maximum possible speed of a peregrine falcon. It is 400km/h when the bird is diving from high in the sky. The highest actual speed ever recorded for a falcon is 389km/h.

steep dive, or stoop, folding back its wings so it plunges head-first at about 250km/h. As it nears the flying target, the falcon sticks out its clenched feet and hits the victim's wing as it rockets past. The impact knocks the bird out of the sky, and as it falls the falcon circles around to catch it in its claws. If the prey is still alive, the falcon kills it with a bite from its hooked beak.

EVOLUTION SOLUTION

Travelling at such great speeds would damage most animals' lungs as air rushes through the nostrils. The peregrine falcon has evolved boney spikes in its nostrils that push the fast-flowing air away.

FACTS AND FIGURES

Scientific name.......... Falco peregrinus
Location.................................... Worldwide
Habitat........... Cliffs, coastlines, cities
Size...50cm
Food................. Pigeons and other birds
Lifespan....................................17 years
Young........... 2 or 3 eggs laid in spring

KOMODO DRAGON

The komodo dragon is the world's biggest lizard. It can kill prey even larger than itself using just a single bite.

Komodo dragons prey on goats and buffaloes, which have been introduced by humans to the dragon's island habitats. Before that, the dragons ate pygmy elephants, which are now extinct. Killing a large animal is not easy. The dragon uses a slow but deadly technique. It sits quietly out of sight, and when prey gets near, it rushes out and delivers a deep bite. The prey is hurt, but able to flee. The lizard plods along behind it, in no rush. Meanwhile, venom in the dragon's saliva stops the bite wound healing, so its prey keeps bleeding. This gradually weakens the victim, and after several days it dies.

FACTS AND FIGURES

Scientific name.. Varanus komodoensis

Location........ Komodo, Flores and other Indonesian islands

Habitat.............................. Forests

Size................................ 2.2–3m

Food... Goats and other large herbivores

Lifespan............................ 50 years

Young... 20 eggs hidden inside burrows

EVOLUTION SOLUTION

Komodo dragons live on a few islands in Indonesia, including their namesake, Komodo Island. The lizards grew to be so large in a process called island gigantism. The species' ancestors were smaller lizards that floated to the islands on drifting tree trunks. When they arrived there were no big hunters living there, and so the lizards evolved to fulfil that role in the food chain.

The deadliest thing about the komodo dragon is its drooling, venomous saliva.

LION

Lions are big cats. They are very similar to tigers. In fact, biologists find it hard to tell a lion skeleton from a tiger's. The tiger is a little larger, but lions are still the best hunting cats, because they hunt as a team.

Lions live in groups called prides. Each pride has about 30 cats, and includes mother lionesses and their cubs, plus a single male lion. The male stops any other adult males from joining the pride, but apart from that the lionesses are in charge. They look after the young and catch all the food.

Lions are nocturnal hunters. By day they laze around in the sun, but as night falls, the cats prepare for a hunting trip. Their main prey are fast-running gazelles. In a straight running race, the gazelle would always beat the lion, so the cats have to use cunning to bring them down.

The hunting party approaches the herd of gazelles from downwind, so their prey cannot smell the lions coming. The male and the cubs

The male lion does not help with the hunt, but gets to eat first. The cubs have to wait until everyone else has finished.

The lion cannot outrun the zebra over a long distance so must bring it down very swiftly.

FACTS AND FIGURES

Scientific name................. Leo panthera

Location......... Africa and western India

Habitat.................Savannahs and forests

Size.. 1.1–1.8m

Food........Antelopes and other mammals

Lifespan....................................... 15 years

Young............... Cub born every 2 years

stay watching on the sidelines, while the lionesses prepare an ambush. One or two sneak around in front of the herd, staying out of sight. More cats spread out in other directions and lie in wait. The first pair then run out of hiding, scaring the gazelles, who run away in the opposite direction – straight into the path of another lioness. She will jump on one gazelle, hauling it to the ground, and then kill it with a bite to the throat.

EVOLUTION SOLUTION

Cats are normally solitary hunters, but to survive on the wide open savannahs of Africa, lions had to evolve another way of hunting their food, and formed a team. Lions are able to change their social system according to where they live. Lions used to live in south-eastern Europe 2000 years ago. It was easier for them to find food here, and they lived in a small family of mother, father and cubs.

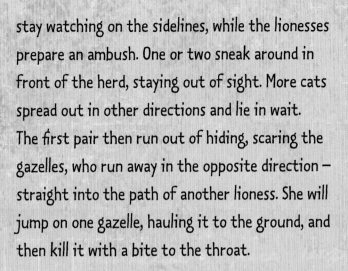

The lions eat the haunches first, and then the liver. They rarely eat the head.

Lions have excellent night vision for tracking prey in the dark.

ANTLION

As an adult, the antlion is a flimsy insect that flutters around looking for a mate. However, in its young, or larval, form it is one of nature's most ruthless killers. As its name suggests, it hunts for ants, building a sand trap for them.

The antlion larva is a tough little bug that lives on beaches or other sandy areas. Two-thirds of it are made up of a plump round body with little legs, the other third is made of the head which is armed with huge pincer-shaped mouthparts. The larva build an ant trap in the sand by going backward around in circles. The plump body is like a sand plough pushing the sand into piles. The insect flicks the sand out of the hole with its flat head. Eventually, the

When an antlion larva is under attack itself, it leaps up into the air and runs off to escape the threat. It leaves tracks in the sand, called doodles.

Antlion larvae glue sand to their body to help stay hidden.

antlion has made a deep pit in the sand, and it buries itself in the centre of it, with just its mighty jaws above the surface. An ant crawling along the surface cannot see the pit and when it falls in, it cannot climb up the steep sandy walls. As it tumbles in, the antlion strikes.

EVOLUTION SOLUTION

Many insects divide their lives between an adult and larval form. The larva looks and behaves very differently to the adult, which prevents them from competing with each other for food or places to live.

FACTS AND FIGURES

Scientific name...................... Myrmeleon
Location..................................... Worldwide
Habitat........... Beaches and sandy areas
Size.. 2–4cm
Food.. Ants
Lifespan...1 year
Young...Eggs scattered on sandy ground

ARGENTINE HORNED FROG

This frog might look harmless, but if you were the size of a mouse, you might think differently. Some people call this amphibian the Pacman frog, because it can swallow its prey in one gulp.

The Argentine horned frog has a body covered in green and black blotches. This helps it hide among the damp leaves that litter the floor of its forest home. The frog buries itself in the leaves so only its eyes are showing. These have little pointed 'horns', completing the leafy disguise. Once in place, the frog waits. Its mouth makes up half of the total body, so when an

A horned frog can eat an animal the same size as itself.

FACTS AND FIGURES

Scientific name.... Ceratophrys ornatai

Location...............................South America

Habitat................................. Woodlands

Size... Up to 15cm

Food.....Frogs, lizards, insects, mammals

Lifespan......................................6–7 years

Young.................. Up to 2,000 eggs laid

insect, mouse or lizard wanders too close – gulp! – the frog strikes. It has tooth-like spikes lining its jaws, which hold the prey as it struggles. The frog then pulls its big eyes into its mouth, so they help force the food down into the stomach.

EVOLUTION SOLUTION

Frogs do not have a neck or throat as such and that means they cannot breathe in and out of their little lungs very effectively. As a result, they take in oxygen through their damp skin – especially the soft lining of the throat. That is one reason why frogs have such big mouths.

A horned frog slowly swallows another frog whole.

KILLER WHALE

Killer whales are sometimes called the 'wolves of the sea'. Like a wolf, these whales are tough enough to survive by themselves, but when they work as a team, nothing can stop them. Even great white sharks fall prey to these mighty hunters.

Also known as orcas, killer whales live and hunt in groups called pods, and each pod has its preferred type of food. Fish-eating pods surround a school of fish, so the fish have nowhere to go. Instead, they are forced to swim in a tighter and tighter ball. Eventually,

EVOLUTION SOLUTION

Killer whales are close relatives of dolphins. The ancestors of dolphins and killer whales evolved to live in complex social groups in which members worked together to find and catch food. The evolution of this social behaviour has made it possible for whale pods to hunt whatever food is available, and that means the whales are able to survive in any part of the world's oceans.

FACTS AND FIGURES

Scientific name.................. Orcinus orca
Location..................................... Worldwide
Habitat...Oceans
Size....................................... 6–9m
Foo........................... Fish, seals, whales
Lifespan.................................50 years
Young..........1 pup born every four years

one of the whales whacks the ball with its wide tail. This stuns most of the fish, which float helplessly in the water while the whales gobble them up.

Killer whales also eat seals. They knock the seal out by giving it a headbutt in the water or even chasing it to a sandy shore and snatching

Killer whale teeth are not very sharp. They are used to crush the food, rather than slice through it.

it in their jaws. Some killer whale pods hunt other whale species. They normally attack calves, which are still bigger than they are. The pod takes it in turns to chase the calf and its mother. After several hours, the prey is exhausted, and the killer whales push the calf underwater, stopping it from coming to breathe at the surface. Within minutes, the calf drowns and the orcas tear into their prey.

The pod sticks together, communicating with calls too high-pitched for humans to hear. The whales can identify each other by the shape of their dorsal fins.

FLOWER MANTIS

The flower mantis's camouflage matches about 20 types of orchid.

Flower mantis have brightly coloured wings that are normally folded out of view. If they are threatened, they fan open their wings, giving the attacker quite a shock.

This insect is a master of disguise. It is so good at pretending to be a flower that no insect can spot it. As soon as its prey gets close, the mantis strikes with lightning speed to snatch it with its spiked arms. There is no escape.

The flower mantis has back legs that are flattened into the shape of petals, while its abdomen looks like a bud about to bloom. However, the insect has another trick to make sure its disguise works even better. When it finds the right flower, it takes up position, holding on with its four back legs. The mantis then begins to sway back and forth, matching the motion of the flowers as they are blown by the breeze. Scientists have found that flying insects collecting nectar and pollen are more likely to land on the mantis than an actual petal!

EVOLUTION SOLUTION

Praying mantises are all ambush hunters that stand so still their victims do not notice them. The flower mantis gradually evolved to match the colour of certain flowers. The mantises that were less easy to see got more food. Eventually, all flower mantises matched the flower colour exactly.

FACTS AND FIGURES

Scientific name..... Hymenopus coronatus
Location........................... Southeast Asia
Habitat................................ Rainforests
Size...4cm
Food............................ Flying insects
Lifespan................................. 1 years
Young...200 eggs laid in case on plants

WOLF

The wolf is the wild relative of our pet dogs. Today, wolves live mostly in remote places, such as cold northern forests or mountain ranges, but they were once common over most of the northern hemisphere. That made them the world's most widespread hunter.

FACTS AND FIGURES

Scientific name.................. Canis lupus
Location................ Northern hemisphere
Habitat..................... Forests and tundra
Size...1–1.6m
Food....... Rabbits, birds, wild boar, deer
Lifespan..................................... 20 years
Young.................... Pack leaders produce 5 or 6 pups each year

EVOLUTION SOLUTION

Wolves are the largest dog species. All dogs have evolved to be incredibly good runners. They have long legs and a big chest filled with a large heart and set of lungs, but they are still quite lightweight. This adds up to an animal that can run all day and all night without getting out of breath.

A wolf is the size of a large pet dog, and by itself it can hunt rabbits and rats. Working as part of a team, or pack, the wolf can get much more food. A pack can bring down large animals, such as a deer. However, this big beast can kill a wolf with a kick or spiked antler, so the wolf pack has to take its time to ensure no one is injured. The pack chases along behind the deer for hours until it becomes too tired to fight back. Then the wolves start to scratch and bite the prey's back, making it even weaker. Finally, one wolf will bite the deer's face until it falls to the ground exhausted. Even if the deer is not dead yet, the wolves start to eat it straight away.

A wolf can run run 60km in one night.

{GLOSSARY}

antennae Sometimes known as feelers, antennae are leg-like structures on the heads of many animals. As well as feeling, antennae are often used for detecting smells.

Arctic The region around the North Pole. The Arctic is always very cold and frequently frozen over.

constriction The act of squeezing something so it stops functioning properly. Many snakes kill prey by constriction.

crustacean A many-legged animal that has an armoured shell. Most crustaceans live in water. The group includes crabs, shrimps and woodlice.

downwind Being located where the wind is blowing smells away from a target animal. Hunters approach from the downwind direction to avoid being detected.

evolution The process by which animals, plants and other life forms change gradually to adapt to changes in their environment.

extinct When all members of a species have died out and so that particular kind of life form disappears.

habitat The kind of environment that an animal lives in. Each species has evolved to survive in its particular habitat.

larva A young form of an insect or other invertebrate. The larva looks different to the adult form and lives in a different way.

mammal A type of animal that grows hairs on its body and produces milk to feed its young.

natural selection The process by which evolution works. Natural selection allows individuals that are good at surviving to increase in number, while those that are less able to compete go down in number.

nocturnal To be active at night.

paralyse To make an animal incapable of moving its body. It is still alive but unable to defend itself.

predator An animal that hunts and kills other animals for food.

prey An animal that is hunted and killed by a predator.

pygmy Something that is smaller than the average size.

silhouette The shadow-like shape of an object.

solution Something that solves a problem.

species A group of animals that share many characteristics. The main feature is that members of a species can breed with each other. Members of different species cannot produce young together successfully.

vacuum A space with nothing in it, not even air.

venom A poison produced by an animal that is pumped into its victims, either by a bite or a sting.

BOOKS

INFOGRAPHIC TOP 10: Record-Breaking Animals,
by Jon Richards and Ed Simkins (Wayland, 2015)

SUPER NATURAL ANIMALS,
by Leon Gray (Wayland, 2014)

WHAT IS EVOLUTION?,
by Louise Spilsbury (Wayland, 2015)

WEBSITES

www.zsl.org/kids-zsl

The kids' section of the Zoological Society of London's website is packed
with animal information, games and activities, as well as the latest
scientific studies.

www.natgeokids.com/uk/

Look for animal-related facts, pictures and games in
the kids' section of the National Geographic website.

www.nhm.ac.uk/visit/activities-for-families-and-kids.html
The Natural History Museum website is filled
with games, facts and information on the world of animals.

INDEX

Published in paperback in Great Britain in 2019 by Wayland
Copyright © Hodder and Stoughton, 2015

All rights reserved.

Editor: Julia Adams
Designer: Rocket Design

Dewey number: 591.5'3-dc23
ISBN 978 1 5263 0766 8

Printed in China

10 9 8 7 6 5 4 3 2 1

Picture acknowledgements: Cover, p. 1: © Anup Shah/naturepl.com; p. 3 © Michael D Kern/naturepl.com; pp. 4–5: © Lou Coetzer/naturepl.com; p. 6 (top): © Chris and Monique Fallows/naturepl.com; p. 6 (bottom): © Doug Perrine/naturepl.com; p. 7: © Alex Mustard/naturepl.com; p. 8: © David Hall/naturepl.com; p. 9: © Anup Shah/naturepl.com; p. 10 (top): © Charlie Hamilton James/naturepl.com; p. 10 (bottom): © Andy Rouse/naturepl.com; p. 11: © Sven Zacek/naturepl.com; p. 12: © Luciano Candisani/FLPA; p. 13: © Emanuele Biggi/FLPA; pp. 14–15: © Suzi Eszterhas/naturepl.com; p. 16: © Steven Kazlowski/naturepl.com; p. 17: © David Shale/naturepl.com; p. 18 (top): © Alex Hyde/naturepl.com; p. 18 (bottom): © Steven Dalton/naturepl.com; p. 19: © Kim Taylor/naturepl.com; p. 20, p. 31: © Konrad Wothe/Minden Pictures/Corbis; p. 21: © Will Burrard-Lucas/naturepl.com; p. 22: © Peter Blackwell/naturepl.com; p. 23 (top): © Denis-Hout/naturepl.com; p. 23 (bottom): © Anup Shah/naturepl.com; p. 24: © Jane Burton/naturepl.com; p. 25: © John Cancalosi/naturepl.com; p. 26–27: © Chris and Monique Fallows/naturepl.com; p. 27: © Brandon Cole/naturepl.com; p. 28: © Michael D. Kern/naturepl.com; p. 29: © David Welling/naturepl.com; all images used as graphic elements: Shutterstock.

The website addresses (URLs) included in this book were valid at the time of going to press. However, it is possible that contents or addresses may change following the publication of this book. No responsibility for any such changes can be accepted by either the author or the Publisher.

Every attempt has been made to clear copyright. Should there be any inadvertent omission, please apply to the publisher for rectification.

Wayland, an imprint of Hachette Children's Group
Part of Hodder & Stoughton
Carmelite House
50 Victoria Embankment
London
EC4Y 0DZ

An Hachette UK Company
www.hachette.co.uk
www.hachettechildrens.co.uk

MIX
Paper from
responsible sources
FSC® C104740